THE
INFOGRAPHIC
GUIDE TO
COLLEGE

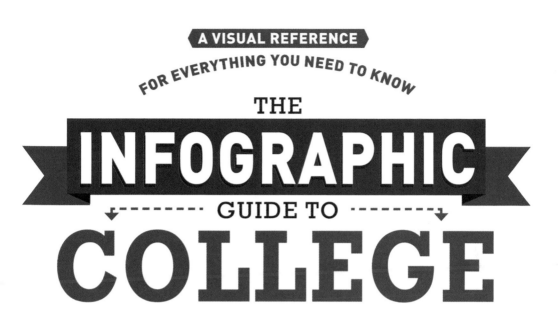

A VISUAL REFERENCE

FOR EVERYTHING YOU NEED TO KNOW

THE
INFOGRAPHIC
GUIDE TO
COLLEGE

Adams Media
New York   London   Toronto   Sydney   New Delhi

Adams Media
An Imprint of Simon & Schuster, Inc.
57 Littlefield Street
Avon, Massachusetts 02322

First Adams Media trade paperback edition JULY 2017

ADAMS MEDIA and colophon are trademarks of Simon and Schuster.

For information about special discounts for bulk purchases, please contact Simon & Schuster Special Sales at 1-866-506-1949 or business@simonandschuster.com.

The Simon & Schuster Speakers Bureau can bring authors to your live event. For more information or to book an event contact the Simon & Schuster Speakers Bureau at 1-866-248-3049 or visit our website at www.simonspeakers.com.

Interior design by Elisabeth Lariviere
Image credits listed at the end of this book

Manufactured in the United States of America

10 9 8 7 6 5 4 3 2 1

ISBN 978-1-5072-0336-1
ISBN 978-1-5072-0483-2 (ebook)

Contains material adapted from the following title published by Adams Media, an Imprint of Simon & Schuster, Inc.: *The Everything® College Survival Book, 3rd Edition* by Susan Fitzgerald and J. Lee Peters, copyright © 2011, ISBN 978-1-4405-1207-0.

Contents

SECTION 1

CAMPUS LIFE

Packing for College • 14

How to Be the Best
Roommate Ever • 16

10 Ideas for Decorating
Your New Space • 18

15 Must-Know Tips
for Staying Safe
at College • 20

Laundry 101 • 22

15 Ways to Avoid the
Freshman 15 • 24

10 Ways to De-Stress
Right Now • 26

A Road Map to an
Amazing Spring
Break! • 28

10 Cleaning Hacks to
Keep Your Room Clean
All Semester • 30

Getting Around
Town • 32

10 Instant Cold
Remedies That
Really Work • 34

Studying Abroad:
A Look at Your
Options • 36

5 Alternative Ways
to Spend Winter and
Spring Breaks • 38

10 Things You Need
to Do Before Living
Off Campus • 40

ACADEMIC SUCCESS

 The Path to Declaring a Major • 44

 The Dos and Don'ts of Picking Classes • 46

 6 Ways to Enhance Your Reading Skills • 48

 A Checklist for Getting the Most Out of Lectures • 50

4 Must-Have Study Tools • 52

 How to Write an A+ Paper: A Checklist • 54

7 Steps to Forming a Successful Study Group • 56

 The Secret to Acing Any Exam • 58

 Presentation Dos and Don'ts • 60

 8 Ways to Build a Professional Relationship with Your Professor • 62

 7 Steps to Dealing with Bad Grades • 64

 8 Easy Steps for Writing a Research Paper • 66

 Exam Week: A Timeline to Acing Tests • 68

SECTION 3

SOCIAL SKILLS

 The Top 10 Places to Meet New People • 72

 6 Ways to Get Involved on Campus • 82

 Building a Relationship with Your RA • 74

 11 Impressive Spots to Take Your Date • 84

 Dos and Don'ts for Managing Conflicts with Roommates • 76

 Drinking Games 101 • 86

10 Ways to Help Out Your Community • 78

 12 Tips for Hosting a Memorable Party • 88

The Truth about Greek Life • 80

 Downing a Drink: What You Need to Know • 90

FINANCIAL AID

$$ Scholarships vs. Grates vs. Loans • 94

 Budgeting 101 • 108

 How to Apply for a Loan • 96

 The Top 7 Part-Time Jobs That Will Help Pay Your Bills • 110

 10 Ways to Save Money in College • 98

?? The Dos and Don'ts of Job Hunting • 112

 What You Need to Know about Credit Cards • 100

 Bring Your College Experience Full Circle with an Internship • 114

 7 Apps to Help You Manage Your Money • 102

 How to Recover from a Spending Binge • 116

 Find Your Place in the College Job Scene • 104

Is Grad School for YOU? • 118

Student Debt by the Numbers • 106

INTRODUCTION

You finally got the acceptance letter you've been waiting for and are getting ready to head to college. Are you nervous? Excited? Wondering how you're going to pull it all off? After all, with everything from roommates to classes to a whole new type of social life, college is a lot to take in.

Fortunately, *The Infographic Guide to College* gives you all the ins and outs of being a college student. And, because you're going to spend so much time with your nose buried in a heavy textbook, here you'll learn everything you need to know from a series of fun, bite-sized, easy-to-understand infographics.

You'll learn about all the necessities of college life, like how to get along with your roommates, do laundry, ace your classes, navigate the financial aid system, get an internship, avoid the Freshman 15, and more. And, because college is about more than academics, you'll also find info on hosting a killer party, getting involved in Greek life, the best spots to take a date, and the rules to some popular drinking games.

Whether you're going to a public or private college, living far from home or in your childhood bedroom, or attending a four-year school or a two-year school, the topics covered throughout the book will help you think about and prepare for the amazing experience that is college. And with a little thought and preparation, the transition to your college years can be a smooth one.

So get ready to make lifelong friends, try new things, excel in your classes, and be challenged to figure out who you really are. Because whether you're just packing up your car for your freshman year, getting ready to live off campus, or trying to decide if grad school is in your future, the colorful images in *The Infographic Guide to College* have got you covered.

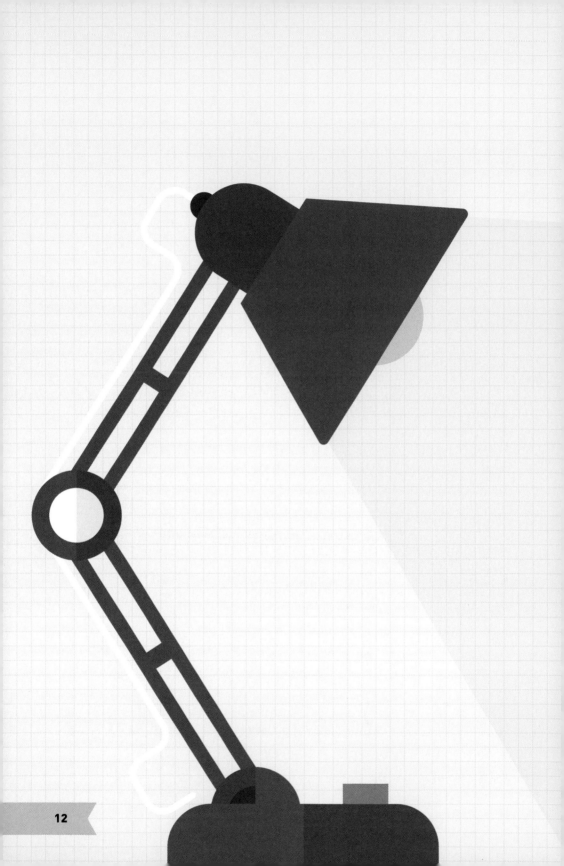

Campus Life

 Packing for College • 14

How to Be the Best Roommate Ever • 16

10 Ideas for Decorating Your New Space • 18

15 Must-Know Tips for Staying Safe at College • 20

 Laundry 101 • 22

15 Ways to Avoid the Freshman 15 • 24

10 Ways to De-Stress Right Now • 26

 A Road Map to an Amazing Spring Break! • 28

10 Cleaning Hacks to Keep Your Room Clean All Semester • 30

 Getting Around Town • 32

10 Instant Cold Remedies That Really Work • 34

Studying Abroad: A Look at Your Options • 36

5 Alternative Ways to Spend Winter and Spring Breaks • 38

10 Things You Need to Do Before Living Off Campus • 40

PACKING FOR COLLEGE

The first things you need to know are the size of your room and how many students will be sharing that space. Since your room will already come with a bed, a desk, and a dresser, you'll want to focus on packing toiletries, clothing, and decorations. Here's a list of must-haves to get you started, but be sure to think creatively and in three dimensions when deciding what to bring.

Hair dryer, if you use one

Toothpaste, dental floss, and mouthwash

Toothbrush and case

Shaving cream and razors

Cotton swabs

Over-the-counter medicine for pain

Nail clippers and file

Deodorant

Shampoo and conditioner

Flip-flops or shower shoes

Contact lens care equipment

Soap and soap dish, preferably covered

Hairbrush or comb

Toiletries

Clothing

Bathing suit

Bathrobe

Sportcoat/tie

Jeans

Rain jacket
and umbrella

Sweatshirts and
sweatpants

Pajamas

Nice dress

Exercise
clothing

T-shirts/long
sleeve shirts

Sweaters

Shoes: sneakers,
sandals, one nice
pair of shoes

COLLEGE

How to Be the

BEST ROOMMATE EVER

EVEN IF YOU'RE COMPLETELY DIFFERENT

. . . .

Your roommate may be the person who wakes you up when you sleep through your alarm and invites you to great parties, or might simply be the person you share a room with for a few months. In any case, this person will be an important figure in your life, so it's important that you build a strong and respectful relationship.

Here's how.

Manage Your Initial Expectations.

Your roommate is probably just as excited and nervous as you regarding college and living together. Be sure to meet up at orientation or connect online ahead of time in order to start getting to know each other.

Don't Pass Judgment.

Try not to make snap judgments about your new roommate based on social network information or the few details you already know. People put up a lot of information online that is specifically targeted to their friends that might lead you to the wrong conclusion.

Get to Know Them.

In addition to asking your roommate about the classes they're taking and what you'll need for move-in day, ask them about themselves. What do they like to do for fun, and what are their future career plans? Finding out more information can help you build a solid foundation for your relationship.

Set Boundaries.

Discuss important issues like cleaning or sharing belongings. Also, address your personalities and schedules, especially if one of you is a night owl who loves having friends over. Setting rules can help make you both more comfortable in your space.

Ask Tough Questions.

Your dorm room belongs to both of you, and whatever happens in it affects both of you. Be sure to discuss alcohol and drugs thoroughly as well as having people over, especially partners. Be honest about your desires and listen carefully to your roommate's views.

Be Prepared to Disagree.

As you get to know each other better, you may find more issues that need to be managed before they become conflicts. Plan to work through your differences, and have honest, private conversations with your roommate. If you're unable to come to an agreement on an issue, don't be afraid to ask your RA for guidance.

10 IDEAS FOR DECORATING YOUR NEW SPACE

So, you're leaving home and beginning a new life. While you might want to pack up everything you own, you should keep in mind that you'll stay in your new place for only nine or ten months. Instead, use this opportunity to transform your new room with just a few essentials. Here are some ideas to help you get started.

1. Bring the outdoors inside with succulents and bamboo plants

2. Build a unique headboard with bold fabric, batting, cardboard, and a staple gun

3. Use washi tape to frame posters or prints on your wall

4. Add a colorful rug to brighten your space

5. Dress up your full-length mirror by painting the frame

6. Pick up fun floor pillows for extra seating

7. Paint mason jars and boxes for one-of-a-kind desk organization

8. Swap out plastic storage bins for colored cloth bins

9. Hang up a geometric or patterned corkboard instead of the standard whiteboard

10. Create a photo wall of your family, friends, and places you've visited

15 ⟨ MUST-KNOW TIPS FOR
STAYING SAFE AT COLLEGE

At college, your safety and well-being will be primarily your responsibility. You may already be security-savvy, or this may be a new reality that you need to adapt to quickly. Much of what you need to know about personal safety seems like common sense, but these tips are worth implementing in order to be as safe and secure as possible while at school.

 1. Lock your residence hall room door when you are out or sleeping.

 2. Try not to overshare your whereabouts on social media.

 **3. Keep cash and valuables hidden in dresser drawers or secured in a small safe in your room.**

! **4. Check with the campus security office before carrying pepper spray.**

! **5. Bring a few friends with you when walking around campus at night.**

6. Be aware of your surroundings and the people nearby.

7. Stay in well-lit areas on main travel routes.

8. Don't carry a lot of cash when you go out.

9. Let a roommate or friend know where you're going and when you expect to return.

10. Make sure you're signed up for the campus emergency notification system.

11. Be familiar with emergency procedures and your school's "low-tech" emergency warning systems.

12. Always leave yourself an out when traveling off campus, such as carrying enough cash for a cab.

13. Take public transportation back to campus if you've been drinking.

14. Never accept a drink that you have not seen poured or opened. Once you've been served, always keep an eye on your drink.

15. Use your cell phone to call 911 if you feel you are in danger.

LAUNDRY
101

It turns out that doing laundry is just a little more complicated than throwing clothes in the washer, adding some detergent, and coming back later to put everything in the dryer. Or rather, it is a little more complicated if you want your clothes to look good and last for a while. In order to keep your clothes in good shape, you'll need to work out a laundry schedule, learn to sort your clothes according to material and color, and organize a laundry budget.

1 A good rule of thumb is to do two loads every week.

LAUNDRY BAG

LAUNDRY BAG

2 Sort your clothing by color and material.

3 Add in a powder or liquid detergent.

* Powder detergent should be added before your clothes. Liquid detergent can be added whenever.

4

Choose a water temperature. Use cold water for dark colors and new clothes, hot water for whites or particularly dirty clothes, and warm water for everything in between.

5

Put your washed clothes in the dryer.

* Add a dryer sheet to soften your clothing and prevent static cling.

* Don't forget to clean out the lint trap!

6

Read a book or study while you wait.

7

Fold or hang your clothing to prevent wrinkles.

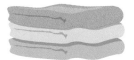

15 Ways to Avoid the

While the Freshman 15 is something that many students worry about, staying healthy doesn't have to be difficult. Use these 15 tips to help you stay on track and ward off future weight gain. It really can be as easy as having a smaller lunch when you have a big dinner date planned or avoiding the dessert line to resist temptation.

1. EXERCISE REGULARLY
Whether you hit the gym or take a class, try to stick to a predictable schedule.

2. PLAN AHEAD
You should try to plan your meals for the whole day to make sure you're getting proper nutrition.

3. FIND A WORKOUT BUDDY
Including a friend in your gym routine can help you hold yourself accountable for your health. Ask a friend to try a new fitness class with you or join you in the gym.

6. SIGN UP FOR A RACE
Whether you're preparing for your first 5K or you're an experienced runner, training for a race will help you get in shape and stick to your fitness goals.

4. CUT DOWN ON COFFEE AND ALCOHOL
While coffee and alcohol may be considered staples for many college students, these potentially high-calorie beverages can also be the cause of weight gain.

5. TRACK CALORIES
Consider using a calorie-tracking app, such as Lose It! or MyFitnessPal, to keep track of not only what you're eating, but how much you're eating throughout the day.

7. EAT BREAKFAST
While skipping breakfast may seem like a good idea when you're rushing to get to class, studies have shown that it may lead to weight gain.

Freshman 15

15. STOCK UP ON HEALTHY OPTIONS
Keep snacks such as fruit, raw veggies and hummus, granola bars, microwave popcorn, and protein bars around.

14. CONTROL YOUR PORTIONS
Each time you make a trip to the serving line or buffet, take only one serving of food. If you are still hungry, you can always return for a second helping.

13. RESIST TEMPTATION
If you know you'll be some-where with unhealthy food, consider bringing one of your snacks with you, so you always have a healthy option.

10. SHARE TAKEOUT ORDERS
Consider splitting delivery orders with friends, or dividing meals and eating the leftovers the next day.

12. GET ENOUGH SLEEP
The truth is that your body needs seven to nine hours of sleep each night, and this amount must be kept relatively consistent in order for you to maintain a healthy weight.

9. DE-STRESS
The next time you feel stress or anxiety, take a break and visit a friend, go for a run, read your favorite book, practice yoga in your room, tune out with music, or meditate.

11. ASK EXPERTS
If you don't know how to begin a healthy weight-loss program, talk to someone at your campus health center or your physician. These experts can help you figure out where to start your health and fitness journey, set appropriate goals, and inspire you to stay on track.

8. DRINK UP
Not only should you be drinking eight glasses of water per day, but you should also try to drink a glass before every meal.

10 WAYS TO DE-STRESS RIGHT NOW

Academic and social pressures can cause stress or anxiety. While these feelings can be overwhelming, the good news is that there are a variety of ways to quickly relax your mind and body.

1 TALK TO A FRIEND

Friends can be a great support system. Don't be afraid to open up to your roommate or other friends about what you're going through.

2 GET ACTIVE

Physical exercise, whether it's achieved through playing a sport or working out at the gym, will release endorphins and dissipate stress.

3 JOT YOUR FEELINGS DOWN IN A JOURNAL

Putting your thoughts and experiences on paper will help you understand what you're feeling and how to move forward.

4 LISTEN TO YOUR FAVORITE TRACKS

Whether you're into heavy metal or indie pop, music will help you forget about your worries and reset your mind.

5 DIVE INTO A BOOK FOR THIRTY MINUTES

Flip open your favorite book and spend thirty minutes seeing the world from a new perspective.

6 EAT A SNACK

Healthy snacks can help you feel grounded and boost your energy. Bananas, in particular, contain potassium which helps you regulate your blood pressure.

7 MEDITATE

Whether you use an app to guide you through a meditation or whip out a coloring book, take some time to shift your focus elsewhere and quiet your mind.

8 GO FOR A WALK

Take a ten-minute walk around your building or campus to change your surroundings and see some friendly faces.

9 TAKE A BREATH

Try this breathing exercise: Breathe slowly through your nose in four-second increments. Deeply inhale, hold your breath, exhale slowly, and then pause for a moment to collect yourself. You can repeat if needed.

10 WATCH CUTE OR FUNNY VIDEOS ONLINE

Viral videos, especially ones with adorable puppies or kittens in them, are instant pick-me-ups.

A ROAD MAP TO AN AMAZING Spring Break!

1 Start thinking about your spring break late in the fall semester. You'll see a lot of information about special spring break vacation packages around that time.

2 Decide what kind of vacation you want to go on. Keep in mind that you'll have several spring breaks during your college career, and you can try different things each time.

3 Choose your travel companions carefully. Everyone must have the same goals for the trip. If your friends want to attend lots of parties and you want to sit on the beach all day, there are bound to be conflicts.

4 Research lodging thoroughly. Ask the company to elaborate on the size, style, and location of the rooms, if the information is not available on their website.

Over the years, you may have developed certain ideas and misconceptions about what your spring break should look like. The truth is that spring break is what you make of it. Luckily, with some research, planning, and a big enough budget, you can transform your break into an amazing vacation.

7 Begin the countdown! Once you've booked your vacation, it's time to count down the days until spring break. Use this time to save a little bit of extra cash for additional expenses.

6 Don't overlook food. It's unlikely that your package will include all meals, but some packages include a continental breakfast or some sort of buffet. Find out what is included and what meals you'll have to provide for yourself.

5 Consider additional travel. While getting to your destination and back may be taken care of, traveling from your hotel to local attractions may be something you have to figure out. If such services are not included in your package be sure to build that expense into your spring break budget.

10 Cleaning Hacks to Keep Your Room Clean All Semester

With all the studying you'll have to do, you won't have time to keep your dorm room immaculate. Luckily, there a few cleaning hacks that can help you spruce up your space fast, whether you're inviting friends over or your parents are coming to visit.

1. Pull the covers over your bed to immediately make your room look cleaner.

2. Keep cotton balls infused with orange essential oil in a bowl to freshen up your space.

3. Use a coffee filter to wipe a dusty laptop or TV screen.

4. Friend got sick on your rug? Clean it up with baking soda and water.

5. Clean crumbs from your keyboard with a sticky note or a toothbrush.

6. Need more room in your fridge? Attach binder clips as a shelf stopper to stack beers.

7. Remove dust from your desk or dresser with an old sock.

8. Heat water and vinegar in a glass cup in the microwave for ten minutes. Then, wipe down the inside with a paper towel—the grime will come right off!

9. Can't keep track of your cables? Keep them organized by threading them through toilet paper rolls.

10. Place an open baking soda box in your fridge to keep smells at bay.

Getting Around Town

The larger the city you're moving to, the more options you'll have as far as shops, restaurants, and other sources of entertainment are concerned. If you're interested in exploring everything your new home has to offer, consider utilizing the following modes of transportation.

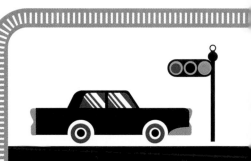

RIDESHARE SERVICES

Companies like Lyft and Uber allow you to seamlessly hail a ride through an app on your phone. Since the app is linked to your credit card, every payment is cash-free and these services rarely require tipping. However, one downside is that the price fluctuates depending on demand.

PUBLIC TRANSPORTATION

If your college is in a city, you'll probably have access to public transportation, including buses and trains. While these modes of transportation can make traveling around easier, they also require planning since they run on specific schedules.

SCHOOL SHUTTLE

Your college may offer a free shuttle that takes students to key places in your area, such as shopping malls or grocery stores. Your student center will be able to provide you with more information on when and where you can find the shuttle.

BICYCLE

Many students take their bicycles with them to school for an easy way to get around. Keep in mind that some colleges may have you register your bicycle, and many cities will require cyclists to follow automobile travel regulations.

CAR

While it may be nice to have a car on campus, it can also be expensive. Not only will your college charge you for having a car, but you may also acquire dents, get parking tickets, and see your insurance go up.

10 Instant Cold Remedies That *Really* Work

While at college, you might notice that you get sick a little more frequently than you did in high school. If you find yourself feeling rundown, here are a few at-home remedies that can help ease cold symptoms and make you feel better in no time.

1 To open your nasal passages, add a few drops of eucalyptus oil to a wash cloth and place the wash cloth on your shower floor where the water hits.

2 Drink ginger tea to ease inflammation and soothe your throat.

3 Stock up on foods with vitamin C or take a supplement.

4 Use a saltwater gargle to soothe a sore throat.

5 Prop up your head with a few pillows to make breathing easier when sleeping.

7 Add raw honey to your tea or eat it by the spoonful.

6 Stay hydrated to loosen congestion.

8 Incorporate peppermint oil into a salve to cool you down and help you breathe easier.

9 Use a humidifier to break up congestion and improve drainage.

10 Use saline nasal sprays to combat stuffiness.

STUDYING ABROAD:

While in school, you can take advantage of the opportunity to visit, study in, and perhaps even live in other parts of the world. Studying abroad gives you the opportunity to study your major from the perspective of another environment and learn more about another culture. Though going abroad can be scary, it can also enrich your life in ways you never thought possible.

A Look at Your Options

SEMESTER AND FULL-YEAR PROGRAMS

- ✗ Most students choose to study abroad for one semester or one academic year.
- ✗ Many colleges have their own study-abroad programs.
- ✗ You'll live at a university, in an apartment, or with a local family.
- ✗ You can fully immerse yourself in the culture.
- ✗ It's helpful if you are proficient in the language of your host country.
- ✗ It gives you the opportunity to get an internship, start a community service project, or tutor local students.
- ✗ You'll need to make sure your financial aid package covers it.
- ✗ The program may count toward your degree and graduation requirements.

SUMMER AND INTERSESSION PROGRAMS

- ✗ This option is very much like an extended class trip.
- ✗ It typically lasts from five to eight weeks.
- ✗ It is offered through your college.
- ✗ The trip may involve traveling to several countries.
- ✗ This program doesn't affect your financial aid package.
- ✗ It's available to students regardless of their declared major.
- ✗ The program may count toward your degree and graduation requirements.

5 ALTERNATIVE WAYS TO SPEND WINTER AND SPRING BREAKS

Deciding what to do during your winter or spring break can be difficult. You'll want to make the most of the experience without spending too much money. If a trip isn't in your budget, you can still have a memorable week. Here are some alternative ideas for a fun and rewarding break.

❶ VISIT NEW FRIENDS

If your new college friends live in a different part of the country, this is an awesome opportunity to see places you've never visited before and try something new. For example, if you're from the south, you could visit someone in the north and go skiing or ice-skating for the first time.

❷ BRING A FRIEND HOME WITH YOU

Alternately, you might decide to bring a friend home with you for break. This will not be as adventurous for you, but you'll have a good time showing them around your city and playing tourist for the week.

➌ HELP THOSE IN NEED

You can use your break to help change the lives of dozens, or even hundreds, of people. Consider working with widely established organizations, such as Habitat for Humanity or United Way, or with local entities, such as an animal shelter or a soup kitchen during your week off.

➍ EARN EXTRA CASH

Since college break periods are rarely more than a week long, it is hard to find good employment during this time. Ask your neighbors if they need help with any odd jobs, such as babysitting or shoveling snow, to earn extra money.

➎ EXPLORE YOUR CAMPUS NEIGHBORHOOD

GALLERY

If you're "stuck" on campus during a break, take day trips to local attractions. Do some research and see if any national parks, historical monuments, or museums are near your campus. It's also worth seeing what shows or other cultural events are taking place in your area during your break period.

10 THINGS YOU NEED TO DO
BEFORE LIVING OFF CAMPUS

1. Begin the apartment hunt early for more options.

2. Check Craigslist or local newspapers for available apartments.

3. Create a checklist for the ideal apartment.

4. Spend time online exploring the apartment's proximity to grocery stores, train stops, and other things you might be interested in.

5. Visit the property before you make a decision.

Renting your own apartment during college will provide you with more independence and more responsibility. There are numerous details to tend to and no office or advisor to help you keep on top of your commitments. Whether you're looking for a cheaper housing option or want to get away from campus, there are some things you should consider doing before signing a lease.

6. Talk to your potential landlord about expectations, especially repairs.

7. Find out how much the security deposit is, and whether you need to sign a lease.

8. Ask your potential landlord for references.

9. Contact each utility company several weeks in advance to arrange for service to your apartment. Ask them about standard utility costs in your area.

10. Keep track of receipts or confirmation emails for your own records.

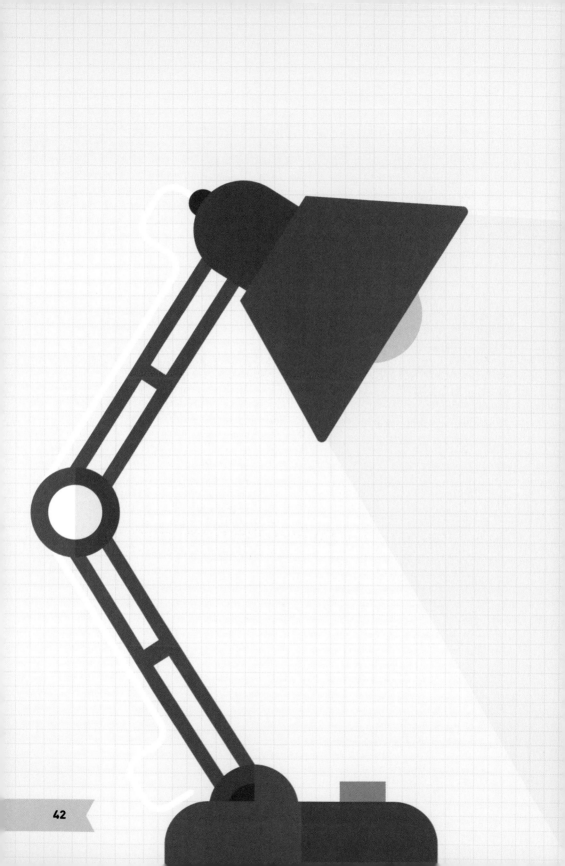

Academic Success

 The Path to Declaring a Major • 44

 The Dos and Don'ts of Picking Classes • 46

 6 Ways to Enhance Your Reading Skills • 48

A Checklist for Getting the Most Out of Lectures • 50

4 Must-Have Study Tools • 52

 How to Write an A+ Paper: A Checklist • 54

 7 Steps to Forming a Successful Study Group • 56

 The Secret to Acing Any Exam • 58

 Presentation Dos and Don'ts • 60

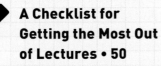 **8 Ways to Build a Professional Relationship with Your Professor • 62**

 7 Steps to Dealing with Bad Grades • 64

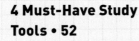 **8 Easy Steps for Writing a Research Paper • 66**

 Exam Week: A Timeline to Acing Tests • 68

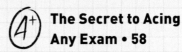

The Path to Declaring a Major

You may have come to college with a career goal in mind, or you may not have any idea what you'd like to do. Luckily, you'll have some time before you need to declare a major, so take that opportunity to find out what excites you.

1

In addition to your core requirements, make sure you take a variety of courses during your first few semesters. Your initial reaction to a class may be one of disdain—how much fun can, for example, a psychology class really be?—but you may find yourself engaged in the subject matter once you take the class. By including a range of courses in your schedule, you'll be better able to develop your interests.

4

Your registrar will have the official major declaration form for you to complete. If you found a subject within your major that you're particularly interested in, you may want to declare a minor at the same time.

2 Visit your career center and ask for their thoughts on appropriate majors as well as potential career paths. They can help you understand how a single major can launch a career in one of several fields, giving you more flexibility and perhaps peace of mind when you declare a major.

3 When you know what your major will be, sit down with your academic advisor and discuss your plans. Your academic advisor can help you figure out which requirements you've already fulfilled for that major, as well as which courses you still need to take.

5 Keep in mind that you must declare your major no later than the end of your second year or the beginning of your third year, depending on the school, but are able to change it until then.

The *DOS* and **DON'TS** *of* PICKING CLASSES

✓ DO

- [ ] Familiarize yourself with the course catalog.

- [ ] Talk to friends who have taken the class or had the professor before.

- [ ] Figure out what kind of tutoring is available for the class or subject matter.

- [ ] Visit your advisor if you have any questions.

- [ ] Pick classes that require different types of work, such as lab time, essay writing, and oral presentations.

- [ ] Register early.

- [ ] Be prepared with a backup list of classes in case some are full.

- [ ] Schedule classes when you're most productive.

- [ ] Consider how your class times fit in with your personal life.

Your academic success really starts with the day you add courses to your schedule, so it's especially important to think about different classes and how you take them on. Depending on who you ask, you'll find a variety of techniques for building out your semester, but these dos and don'ts can help you figure out what options will set you up for success.

☒ DON'T

☐ Double-book yourself.

☐ Load up your schedule with challenging classes.

☐ Be afraid to try something new.

☐ Sign up for morning classes when you're a night owl, and vice versa.

☐ Overlap classes—it takes time to travel from one class to another.

☐ Postpone your general education requirements.

☐ Rely solely on rating websites like Rate My Professors.

☐ Forget about your major's requirements.

☐ Overlook additional materials or time needed for a class, such as labs.

6 Ways to Enhance Your Reading Skills

While you may have done a lot of reading in high school, you'll have to hone your reading skills yet again in college. Here, you'll be expected to read a lot more material in a much shorter amount of time. The information you read will also reappear on tests, in class discussions, and in the papers you write, so it's important to get the most out of your reading.

1. PICK THE BEST READING SPOT.

Never read in bed. Instead, find a well-lit room that allows you to sit upright either at a desk or table.

2. READ THROUGH THE BOOK.

Read the material completely without taking notes or making marks in your book. You'll need to get a good sense of it all before evaluating what is or is not important.

3. KEEP SPECIFIC QUESTIONS IN MIND.

Your professor has a reason for requiring this reading, and if you can identify this reason ahead of time, you'll get more out of the reading. This kind of intentional reading will help you learn things more quickly.

4. HIGHLIGHT KEY POINTS.

Go back through the material and highlight or underline key points. Highlighting too much is not helpful, so be very selective when doing this.

5. WRITE IN THE MARGINS.

Don't be afraid to take notes in your book. Write down quick questions, points that connect to lectures, or a few words about how you can use the information.

6. REREAD THE MATERIAL A SECOND OR THIRD TIME.

Reviewing the material in your book a few more times can help you understand the concepts better. It can also help you create better notes for writing papers or studying for exams.

A CHECKLIST FOR GETTING
THE MOST
OUT OF LECTURES

Some college professors have attendance policies, but many don't. However, attending lectures is the only way to find out what material your professor finds important and exactly what goes down during class. Whether you're in a classroom or lecture hall, here's how you can set yourself up for success.

IN THE CLASSROOM

☐ Attend every class.

☐ Arrive to your classroom five or ten minutes before the class begins.

☐ Sit in the first three or four rows of the class.

☐ Limit distractions by turning off your phone or instant messaging program.

☐ Briefly review your notes from the last class meeting.

☐ Check your syllabus to get an idea of what will be covered that day.

☐ Participate in discussions.

TAKING NOTES

☐ Include the date and overall topic.

☐ Try to identify and write down the focus of the lecture.

☐ Listen for keywords such as "for example" that indicate important points or transitions.

☐ Watch and listen for nonverbal clues about what is important.

☐ Leave the right quarter of the page as a margin for questions.

☐ Highlight material that will be covered on a test.

☐ Jot down references to textbooks or other sources.

☐ Take notes in outline or bullet form, relying on single-line entries.

☐ Use abbreviations to increase your note-taking speed.

IF YOU MISS CLASS

☐ Ask your professor what material was covered and if there were any handouts.

☐ Talk to other students to find out what you missed.

☐ Ask to copy another student's notes from that day.

4 MUST-HAVE STUDY TOOLS

Keeping up with lectures can be difficult, especially if you're taking a variety of classes. Luckily, there are a number of tools available to help you grasp the material covered in lectures and make the most out of your study sessions. Use this list to find a method that works best for you.

1. INDEX CARDS

- Inexpensive and easy to use for a quick review
- Small enough to fit easily in your bookbag or pockets
- Include key phrases or concepts from class notes and textbooks
- Help you organize your thoughts when studying
- Can be used as flashcards to quiz yourself on the material

2. OLD TESTS AND QUIZZES

- One of the most valuable study tools available
- Can indicate your professor's preferred format for exams
- Show you the concepts your professor focuses on
- Reveal concepts and themes you've struggled with in the past

3. REVIEW SESSIONS

- Will be organized or approved by your professor
- Typically led by a graduate student, teaching assistant, or tutor
- Help you review key concepts and materials
- Give you the opportunity to ask questions about points that are unclear
- Can be a lecture, which focuses on questions, or discussion, which gives everyone a chance to express their thoughts about the topic
- Allow you to compare session material to your study notes to see what you're missing

4. PRACTICE TESTS

PRACTICE TEST

- More advanced study preparation for when you have a good grasp of the material
- Can get a different perspective on your test answers by enlisting the help of a study partner
- Will outline what you think is important from your notes, textbooks, and review sessions
- Will be created using the format your professor is likely to use
- Can also help you further your study materials with multiple-choice tests or vocabulary reviews

How to Write an A+ Paper:

A CHECKLIST ☑

One of the most intimidating sights for a college student may be a blank piece of paper or the blinking cursor on an empty computer screen. You'll likely sit at your desk, surrounded by notes and sources, only to find yourself wondering where to begin. Luckily, this checklist can help you not only get started, but also create a paper worthy of a high grade.

- ☑ Start with the section you feel most confident about.

- ☑ For persuasive papers, begin by writing your conclusion first.

- ☑ Use your own words and cite sources to avoid plagiarism.

- ☑ Save your work every five minutes or so, even if your program autosaves.

- ☑ Save a copy to your college's shared drive, so you can access it from anywhere.

- ☑ Step back from your writing for a few hours or days before reading your rough draft.

- ☑ When reviewing, look at your main ideas and decide whether they adhere to your thesis statement.

- ☑ Look for and fix spelling errors, poor sentence structure, and punctuation mistakes.

- ☑ Trust your dictionary and style guide over your computer's spellcheck feature.

- ☑ Read your paper out loud to find errors.

- ☑ Review your work several times before turning it in.

- ☑ Turn to your college's writing center if you need help or someone to review your work.

- ☑ Keep your work as long as you're in college since your paper may come in handy in the future.

7 STEPS TO FORMING A SUCCESSFUL STUDY GROUP

Studying with classmates can be an effective method of learning material for an exam. If you exercise discipline, you can greatly advance your understanding of a topic and enhance your performance in a class. Use these steps to help you create an effective study group.

1 Gauge your classmates' interest in a study group before or after class.

2 Select one to three other students to join your study group.

3 Choose a location that is accessible and comfortable.

Be prepared and bring study materials. **4**

Start your study sessions with a specific purpose in mind. **5**

Work as a team to make sure everyone learns the material thoroughly. **6**

Make sure everyone contributes to the discussion. **7**

The Secret to Acing Any Exam

If you want to truly succeed on your exams, you need to know more than just the subject matter covered in your course—you need to know what type of exam your professor will give. This will determine how you study and help you best prepare for any exam.

Tips for Essays or Short-Answer Questions

* Be ready to explain concepts covered in class

* Review vocabulary to show you understand the subject matter

* Identify themes in your notes that your professor spoke about at length

* Outline your answers on scrap paper before writing them down

* Create a thesis that's a variation on the exam question

* Include an introduction and concise conclusion

* Always proofread your answers

PASS

IDEA!

Tips for Mulitple-Choice Questions

- ❑ Remember that they often include vocabulary definitions and specific facts

- ❑ Always read through the whole exam before starting to answer questions

- ❑ Start with the section that will be easiest for you

- ❑ Check the grammatical structure of the answers provided and make sure your choice fits the question

- ❑ Keep in mind that vague answers tend to be incorrect

- ❑ If two alternatives are opposites, one of them is probably correct

- ❑ If two choices overlap, both are probably wrong (if there is only one correct answer)

- ❑ If two items are correct, then "all of the above" is probably correct

- ❑ "Always" and "never" tend to appear in incorrect answers

- ❑ Correct answers sometimes repeat some of the terms in the question

- All of the above

Presentation Dos and Don'ts

DO get a good night's sleep.

DO dress nicely, even if your professor doesn't specifically grade for it.

DO rehearse your presentation out loud at least once.

DO try to look around the room and keep eye contact with your audience as much as possible.

DO make sure you have a backup plan in case your computer fails.

DO let your personality shine and share relatable examples.

At some point, your professors may ask you to deliver a presentation in class. While the structure of such presentations varies greatly from class to class, there are a few tips that will help you, no matter the subject matter.

DON'T think you can just wing it.

DON'T go off on a tangent. While a few examples can be helpful, you should keep your presentation focused.

DON'T forget to prepare for questions. You should be ready to explain what you are talking about on the spot.

DON'T write out your presentation word for word on your notecards or in your slides. Stick to briefly outlining what you'll be talking about.

DON'T read off of your notecards or computer screen.

DON'T go overboard. Be sure to keep your presentation, including any visuals you provide, simple and concise.

8 Ways to Build a Professional Relationship with Your Professor

Many new students are intimidated by college professors. However, your professors are your best allies—as long as you build a meaningful relationship with them.

1. Say hi to your professor when he or she enters the room.

2. Participate in class discussions even when no one else is speaking up.

3. Show genuine interest by approaching your professor with questions.

 **4.** Have a quick conversation with your professor in informal settings.

 5. Ask your professor questions that are unrelated to course material.

 **6.** Participate in departmental activities.

 **7.** Share related events or news with your professor.

 **8.** Speak to him or her ahead of time if you'll be missing a class.

7 STEPS TO DEALING WITH BAD GRADES

College is a completely different experience than high school, both in and out of the classroom. You may find that classes are more difficult and move more quickly, that professors expect more from students, and that your old study habits won't be adequate if you want to earn good grades. If you find that you're not getting the grades you want, there are a few things you can do to improve your performance.

1

Review your graded test or paper—without judging yourself.

2

Note the questions, wrong answers, or feedback that surprised you.

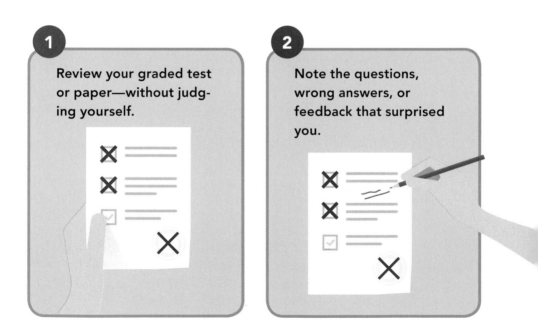

3

Think about how you prepared for the test or paper, and how you could improve your process.

4

Find the answers you missed and work on relearning that material.

5

Talk to your professor to get suggestions on what you could be doing differently.

6

Consider finding a tutor or visiting your advising center for help.

7

Join a study group prior to your next exam or paper to see what topics they focus on.

8 Easy Steps for Writing a Research Paper

The ability to do research and present findings in a professional manner is a foundation of the modern college education. While the process can seem endless, from developing your topic and doing research to writing it out, it doesn't have to be. Use these eight steps to simplify the process and break it down into easily achievable tasks.

1. Choose a Topic

Sometimes a topic will be assigned to you, but most of the time you'll have to propose one to your professor. Pick one that relates back to the class somehow and that you're able to find plenty of information on.

2. Write a Thesis Statement

A thesis statement should be simple and to the point. It should state what you're trying to prove or convey in your paper.

3. Create an Outline

Think of your outline as a table of contents for your paper. It will show anyone, at a glance, what the paper will cover, and should include an introduction, three or four main points, and a conclusion.

4. Start Researching

The library is the place where you'll conduct your research. Most schools have placed their catalogs into searchable databases that streamline research. With these systems, you're able to search by author, title, subject, or keyword.

5. Keep Track of Sources

You'll have to provide a citation each time you use someone else's ideas, and you'll likely have to include a list of the sources you used when you turn in your paper. Many students use index cards to keep track of sources and quotes.

6. Get Help from Your Professor

Don't be reluctant to ask your professor questions or for suggested sources. They may be willing to point you in the right direction or recommend some specialized resources.

7. Pass in a Rough Draft

Many professors will expect to see a rough draft before you have finished your paper. Their feedback and corrections will help you create a better paper and will ensure that you're writing to their specific expectations.

8. Make Revisions and Turn It In

Take your professor's feedback into account when revising your research paper. Before turning it in, make sure you have someone else read through it to check for spelling, grammar, and clarity.

EXAM WEEK:
A Timeline to Acing Tests

It's finally here—exam week! Luckily, you won't have classes to attend, so your open schedule should give you plenty of time to study. But what can you do to make sure you're getting the most out of this time? Use this simple timeline to plan your week.

WEEKEND BEFORE EXAM WEEK

- Fill in your blank schedule with exam and mealtimes.

- Schedule specific study blocks for each exam.

DURING EXAM WEEK

- Review your notes and identify concepts your professor spent time on.

- Create a master study sheet using your notes.

- Schedule time to meet with your study group.

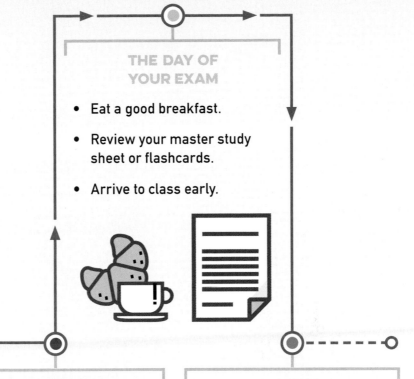

THE DAY OF
YOUR EXAM

- Eat a good breakfast.

- Review your master study sheet or flashcards.

- Arrive to class early.

THE NIGHT BEFORE
YOUR EXAM

- Get a good night's sleep.

- Set your alarm and give yourself plenty of time to get ready in the morning.

DURING
YOUR EXAM

- Answer easy questions first, and then move on to challenging questions.

- If you finish early, go back and review everything.

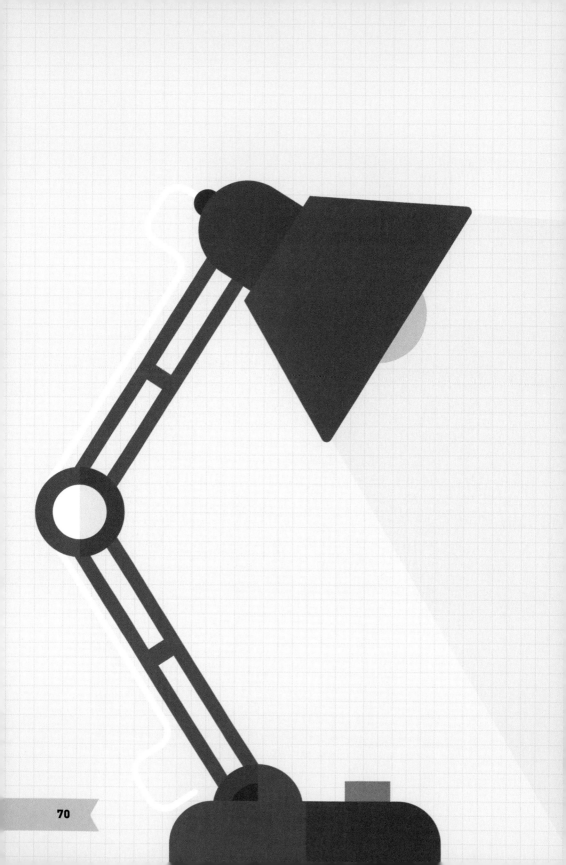

SECTION 3

Social Skills

 The Top 10 Places to Meet New People • 72

 6 Ways to Get Involved on Campus • 82

Building a Relationship with Your RA • 74

 11 Impressive Spots to Take Your Date • 84

Dos and Don'ts for Managing Conflicts with Roommates • 76

 Drinking Games 101 • 86

 10 Ways to Help Out Your Community • 78

12 Tips for Hosting a Memorable Party • 88

The Truth about Greek Life • 80

Downing a Drink: What You Need to Know • 90

The Top 10 Places to Meet New People

After the initial excitement of move-in day and your first few classes has died down, you will probably want to get involved in college activities and meet some new people. Check out these ten spots. They're perfect for socializing with others on campus!

1 Out on the Quad

2 Your Residence Hall

3 The Dining Hall

4 Your Favorite Study Spot

5 Club or Campus Gatherings

6 College-Sponsored Activities

7 On Social Media

8 The Gym or Fitness Classes

9 Parties

10 Your On-Campus Job

Building a Relationship with Your RA

Too often, RAs are stereotyped as cruel enforcers of college policy. Though they do have the unpleasant responsibility of keeping order in raucous residence halls, RAs are just students doing their best to complete requirements and graduate with degrees. Consider these ways to stay on your RA's good side.

SAY HI!

A simple hello when you pass by your RA's room or bump into him or her in the hall will go a long way when it comes to becoming friends.

Attend Their Events

A big part of an RA's job is organizing activities and programs for the residents on their floor or building. Consider attending these events to show that you appreciate their efforts.

Find Common Interests

Be sure to ask your RA about his or her interests the next time you strike up a conversation. You may find that you both love the same bands or have similar hobbies.

HELP PLAN AN EVENT

Don't be afraid to offer suggestions to your RA—in fact, he or she will probably appreciate your ideas.

Follow the Rules

Most RAs are required to report incidences of alcohol consumption, property destruction, and excessive noise on their floors. Be respectful of your peers, your RA, and your building, and you will get along fine.

DOS AND DON'TS FOR
MANAGING CONFLICTS
WITH ROOMMATES

DO

Rehearse what you want to say beforehand.

Sit down with your roommate as soon as possible to discuss the issue.

Keep an open mind and consider alternative solutions.

Explain your views and why the situation upset you so much.

Be concise and focus on the problem at hand.

Listen to your roommate and acknowledge his or her feelings.

Take a break if either of you becomes upset while discussing the situation.

Enlist help from your RA if you're having a hard time confronting your roommate or the situation worsens.

During your first few weeks of college, you and your roommate may get along perfectly. But before long, academic stresses, conflicting schedules, boyfriends and girlfriends, or a lack of space may begin to complicate things. Whether the conflict occurred because someone put an empty milk carton back in the fridge or one roommate borrowed the other's laptop, every issue needs to be resolved.

DON'T

Address the issue if either you or your roommate are heated; instead, take time to calm down.

Let things fester for long before you bring up the issue or continue your conversation.

Interrupt your roommate.

Take a disagreement as an opportunity to address pet peeves.

Drag mutual friends into your disagreements.

Complain to other friends about what is happening since they may repeat your harsh words.

Be defensive or overreact.

Accuse your roommate of anything.

10 WAYS

TO HELP OUT YOUR COMMUNITY

1. Park Cleanup Programs

2. Literacy Programs

3. Homeless Shelters

4. Food Banks or Soup Kitchens

5. Big Brothers Big Sisters

You might already have experience with community service before coming to college. It might have been required as part of your high school curriculum, or maybe you chose to do it on your own. Whether you're seeking similar opportunities or are interested in trying something new, community service is a great way to give back to those who need it most. Here are some programs and organizations to consider.

6. Animal Shelters

7. Domestic Violence Shelters

8. Public Libraries

9. Recycling Programs

10. Habitat for Humanity

THE TRUTH ABOUT
GREEK LIFE

ADVANTAGES
OF GREEK MEMBERSHIP

Gain Lifelong Friendships

Fraternity and sorority members often share similar values, goals, and interests. While participating in Greek activities, you'll get to know your brothers or sisters and will develop a deep bond with them.

Tap Into an Alumni Network

In addition to your fellow members, each campus chapter will have alumni who are eager to assist you during your college years and beyond. When you're looking for an internship or a job and need to make professional connections, these alumni networks can be invaluable.

Develop Leadership Skills

As a member, you'll have the chance to hold a meaningful office and help direct your organization. You'll also benefit from student-to-student mentoring and possibly from alumni mentoring.

Participate in Community Service Opportunities

Many chapters have a particular cause or agency that they work closely with throughout the course of the year. Such service translates into valuable experience, good citizenship, and important parts of a resume.

Encompasses Academic Support

Some chapters maintain study libraries complete with lecture notes or test guides for specific classes or professors. Many chapters will organize study groups for members taking the same class, and often an older member who has already had that class can serve as a tutor.

Fraternities and sororities are among the best known social orga nizations on any college campus. While you may have heard quite a few stories about what goes on inside fraternity and sorority houses, these organizations can offer valuable experience. Choosing to join a Greek organization is a big decision and one that you should consider carefully.

DISADVANTAGES
OF GREEK MEMBERSHIP

Requires a Time Commitment

You'll be expected to participate in a wide variety of activities and attend all formal functions. If you're actively involved in other campus organizations or intercollegiate athletics, you may find it hard to manage all of your commitments in addition to your academic responsibilities.

Brings about Judgment

You may be judged or looked down upon for joining a fraternity or sorority. Unfortunately, there are certain stereotypes associated with Greek life that many people can't look past no matter which organization you join.

Requests Dues

These funds help pay for chapter insurance, membership materials, and other educational resources. Even if you can manage the dues, you'll be expected to pay for other things during your membership, such as special events or gifts for your big brother or little sister.

Involves Hazing

Though virtually every state, school, and national Greek organization has rules prohibiting hazing, forms of it still take place on most campuses. It is difficult for colleges to catch much of the hazing that occurs, and students who deeply desire membership in a particular organization are often reluctant to say "no" to dangerous or humiliating activities.

6 Ways to Get Involved on Campus

Many schools offer a variety of ways to get involved on campus, including familiar clubs like choir and newspaper, as well as others you may have never even heard of. Joining a campus organization allows you to explore different interests, and gives you a chance to meet new people and contribute to a cause.

1. ACADEMIC GROUPS

Each academic department usually has an affiliated club advised by a professor. These groups exist not only for students in the major, but also students who have a casual interest in these subject areas. They might have discussions or go on trips. For example, the biology club may visit a state park to examine plants and animals in the area, as well as enjoy the scenery.

2. ART CLUBS

Your college may also have a group of students who are interested in artistic expression. They may focus on specialty areas, such as singing, painting, and dance, or group themselves as one large organization. These art-expression groups tend to be very active on campus and may sponsor shows or take members to events in the local area.

3. STUDENT GOVERNMENT

Whether or not you participated in student government during high school, your college will welcome your participation in the formal and informal groups that govern student life on campus. The most obvious group to look for is your student senate, but your school may also have building councils that discuss issues in residence halls, or peer discipline boards.

4. PROGRAMMING AND ACTIVITIES BOARDS

Your student activities office will have opportunities for students to join programming boards for big concerts, fall and spring festivals, homecoming events, and other specialized entertainment and cocurricular events, such as lectures and exhibitions.

5. INTRAMURALS

You'll see advertisements for intramural sports programs in your school newspaper, posted online, or at the sports center. When you see one that interests you, register as a team with your friends, or join a team that needs additional players. You'll get the opportunity to play and have fun, as well as meet new people.

6. CLUB SPORTS

Many colleges have club sports available, either to meet a special interest or to fill a gap where an intercollegiate team is not available. Examples of club sports include fencing, crew, and rugby. These clubs give you the opportunity to play a sport you love or learn a sport that is new to you, and are typically less time-consuming than other athletic endeavors.

11 Impressive Spots to Take Your Date

Your college campus is full of fun and easy dating opportunities. From historical parks to shops and quaint cafés, your campus is surrounded by opportunities for you to get out and try new things. The best part is that many of these activities may be free or offered at a discount for students. When you have found someone you want to get to know better, consider these activities:

1. See a movie at a local theater

2. Attend a school sporting event

3. Pack a picnic and go hiking at a park

4. Host a game night

6. Visit a local coffee shop or restaurant

5. Go geocaching

7. Volunteer together in your community

8. Stop by a local museum or a campus art show

9. Go stargazing on campus or at a park

10. Take a tour of the nearest brewery

11. Join a college-sponsored trip to regional attractions

DRINKING GAMES 101

Parties give you a chance to escape the rigors of classes and meet new people. You'll also get the opportunity to showcase your drinking skills with popular games like beer pong and flip cup. Here's the lowdown on the top drinking games played on college campuses.

Beer Pong

1. Rack 10 red plastic cups into triangular formations on either side of a table.
2. Fill each cup with a few ounces of beer.
3. Take turns tossing a ping pong ball into the opposing team's cups.
4. If someone gets a ping pong ball in a cup, the opposing team needs to drink its contents and remove the cup from the table.
5. Continue taking turns, and if necessary, re-racking the cups as they are removed from the table.
6. Whoever clears the cups from the opposing side first is the winner.

Flip Cup

1. Line up two teams of equal players on either side of a table.
2. Each player gets a red plastic cup filled with beer.
3. The first two opposing players should drink their beer and try to flip the empty cup without touching its sides.
4. When the cup lands top up on the table, the next player on the team should repeat the process with their beer.
5. Whichever team has all of its members drink and flip the fastest is the winner.

Quarters

1. Place a glass in the center of a table.
2. Take turns trying to flip a quarter into the cup.
3. If a player is able to get the quarter in the cup, they should command another player to drink.
4. The same player should also create new rules to follow when ordering others to drink.
5. If someone violates a rule, they have to drink.
6. Continue the game until players no longer want to drink and are then disqualified.
7. The last remaining player is the winner.

King's Cup

1. Take the Jokers out of a deck of cards.
2. Create rules for each of the remaining cards.
3. Place a cup in the center of a table.
4. Spread the cards face down around the cup.
5. Players should draw a card and perform the predetermined action during each turn.
6. The first three people to pick a King card should pour some of their drink into the cup in the center of the table.
7. The game ends when someone picks the last King card. This person loses and should drink whatever is in the cup.

12 TIPS FOR HOSTING A MEMORABLE PARTY

While the type of party you host will depend on your budget and space, there are still a few things you'll need to consider doing or including if you want to throw a killer party.

1 Invite all of your friends.

2 Make sure you have enough cups and shot glasses for everyone.

3 Buy plenty of booze and chasers, if your budget allows for it. Otherwise, let people know it's BYOB.

4 Whip up a few batches of Jell-O shots to share with your guests.

5 Create an upbeat playlist that includes songs your friends love.

6 Offer a variety of snacks that guests can easily grab while holding a drink.

7 Introduce your friends to other friends they may not know to cut out any awkwardness.

8 Mingle with everyone throughout the night.

9 Decorate your apartment or dorm room, especially if you have a certain theme, like '80s night.

10 Send out reminders via social media, text, or email several days before the party.

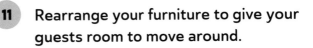

11 Rearrange your furniture to give your guests room to move around.

12 Entertain your guests with party games like flip cup or beer pong.

Downing a Drink: What You Need to Know

Chances are you'll be invited to several parties during the year. While college drinking is often depicted by keg stands and raging parties, it's also possible to have fun and drink alcohol responsibly. Here are some tips and things you should know when downing your drink.

Never drink on an empty stomach.

Always keep track of how much you're drinking.

One beer, a glass of wine, and a one-ounce shot of liquor each contain the same amount of alcohol.

It takes your body one hour to process one ounce of alcohol.

Keep in mind that different drinks are usually consumed at different paces. While a beer is sipped over time, a shot is usually consumed all at once. Four shots in one hour will be more difficult for your body to manage than four beers in four hours.

Carbonated beverages can get alcohol into your system more quickly than noncarbonated beverages.

Your weight and body fat also affect how your body processes alcohol. Heavier people can usually drink more without feeling the effects of alcohol. However, a person with high body fat will feel the effects of alcohol more quickly than a person of similar body type who has less body fat.

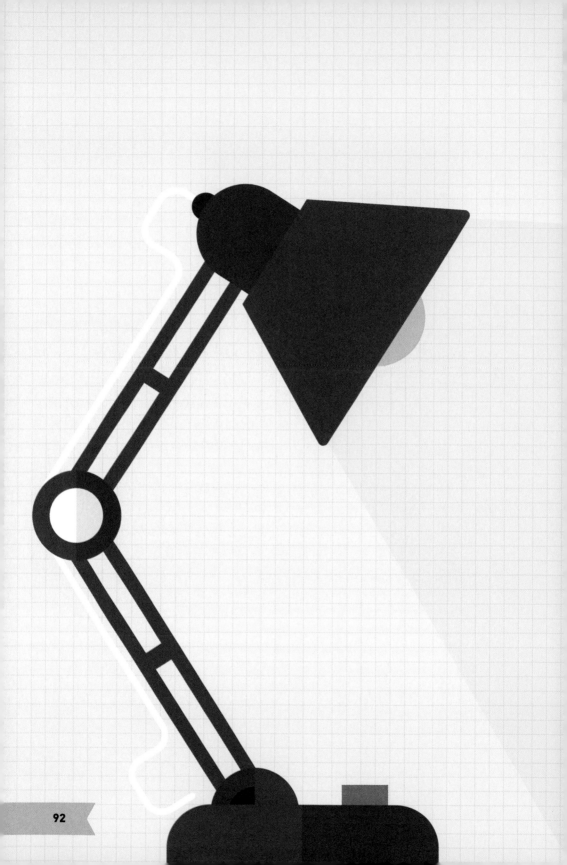

SECTION 4

Financial Aid

$$ Scholarships vs. Grants vs. Loans • 94

Budgeting 101 • 108

How to Apply for a Loan • 96

The Top 7 Part-Time Jobs That Will Help Pay Your Bills • 110

10 Ways to Save Money in College • 98

?? The Dos and Don'ts of Job Hunting • 112

What You Need to Know about Credit Cards • 100

Bring Your College Experience Full Circle with an Internship • 114

7 Apps to Help You Manage Your Money • 102

How to Recover from a Spending Binge • 116

Find Your Place in the College Job Scene • 104

Is Grad School for YOU? • 118

Student Debt by the Numbers • 106

Scholarships vs. Grants vs. Loans

Now that you've completed filling out college applications, it's time to figure out how you're going to pay for that education. Use these methods to get the funds needed to see you through several years of college.

SCHOLARSHIPS

- Defined amounts of money from the government, your college, or an organization

- Don't have to be repaid

- Eligibility is based on academic merit, declared major, alumni relationship, and extracurricular involvement

- Can be found through a quick search for "college scholarships"

- May need to reapply for every year (although some cover all four years)

- There may be strings attached, such as maintaining a particular GPA or continuing in a particular field of study

- May need to complete an essay or interview in addition to an application

GRANTS

- Defined amounts of money from the government, your college, or an organization

- Don't have to be repaid

- Eligibility is usually based on financial need

- Will need to reapply for every year

- May need to complete an essay or interview in addition to an application

LOANS = $$

- A component of almost every financial aid package

- Need to be repaid and usually with interest

- There are only two different types: subsidized and unsubsidized loans

- Eligibility can be either based on financial need or need-blind

- Will need to reapply for every year

- Must complete an entrance interview to learn about your rights and responsibilities

How to Apply for a Loan

You may find that scholarships and grants aren't enough to cover your college education. Loans can help you receive additional aid and it's pretty easy to apply.

Here's how:

1

Complete a Free Application for Federal Student Aid (FAFSA) online early in the calendar year. This form helps colleges determine your expected family contribution and need.

2

Give your school a signed copy of your—and your parents'—tax returns. If your parents are separated or you have other special circumstances, get in touch with your financial aid officer to find out what's needed.

3

Contact your college financial aid office to ask questions and see if there are any other required forms you need to complete. Financial aid officers have an excellent understanding of student needs, federal regulations, and the paperwork necessary to receive financial aid.

4

If you need more financial aid, decide what other options are available and fill out the paperwork for those educational loans.

5

Complete an entrance interview to learn about your rights and responsibilities. Your school may offer a group interview, you may be able to do this with a financial aid counselor, or you may be able to do this online.

$$$

Stafford Loans, which can be subsidized or unsubsidized, and subsidized Perkins Loans are common low-interest loans available to students. Which one is right for you?

SUBSIDIZED LOANS

Subsidized loans are based on the difference between the cost of your education and what you're able to cover. The government will pay the interest on the subsidized loans while you are in college or during grace periods.

UNSUBSIDIZED LOANS

Unsubsidized loans are available to students regardless of individual or family need in relation to the cost of the college. The interest accrues while you are in school, and any unpaid interest rolls over and is added to your loan principal.

10 Ways to Save Money in College

Now that you're in charge of providing everything beyond your basic necessities, you need to establish a budget and find ways to save money. Luckily, saving money doesn't have to mean eating ramen for every meal. Here are a few ideas that will help you cut back on your spending.

3. Split delivery orders with friends or others in your residence hall.

4. Clip and collect coupons for your supermarket.

2. Look for discounts for college students.

1. Consider store-brand items instead of name brands when grocery shopping.

5. Keep track of which restaurants offer weekly or nightly specials.

7. Skip the overpriced latte and invest in a simple coffeemaker (if your dorm allows it).

6. Invest in resealable containers to keep food from spoiling too quickly.

8. Buy food in bulk and divide it into single servings.

9. Take advantage of free campus activities, like movie nights, concerts, or sporting events.

10. Borrow textbooks or buy them used.

WHAT YOU NEED TO KNOW
ABOUT CREDIT CARDS

When you first start college, you may consider applying for a credit card. After all, they come in handy during emergencies and can help you build your credit. However, there are a number of pitfalls as well. Here's what to look out for when choosing and using a credit card.

Always READ THE FINE PRINT in contracts and be wary of offers with free gifts.

The lower your FIXED APR, the better it is for your budget.

Be sure to look at ANNUAL FEES since many cards charge you for using their services.

Plan on getting only ONE CARD, and find one with a LOW CREDIT LIMIT, such as $1,000.

Try not to carry your card with you at all times to AVOID MAKING IMPULSIVE PURCHASES.

Most credit cards allow you to make charges or get CASH ADVANCES.

Cash advances are usually subject to a TRANSACTION FEE and sometimes a HIGHER INTEREST RATE.

Remember that charging something INCREASES ITS COST if you don't pay your bill immediately.

Any time you borrow money or use credit, your CREDIT RATING IS AFFECTED.

Missing payments or CARRYING A LARGE BALANCE can hurt your credit rating.

There are nonprofit agencies that can help you UNDERSTAND YOUR CREDIT REPORT at no cost.

7 APPS TO HELP YOU MANAGE YOUR MONEY

One of the most difficult challenges you'll face while in school is managing your money. After all, there are books to buy, events to go to, and of course, drinks to be had. These seven apps can help make saving money and managing your finances a little easier.

1. MINT

One of the most popular apps for budgeting, Mint keeps track of all your financial accounts and transactions, so you can visualize how much you spend and where you may be able to cut back.

2. VENMO

Never worry about owing your roommate pizza money again! Venmo makes paying back friends and family a breeze by allowing you to instantly transfer funds via your phone for free.

3. LEARNVEST

Like Mint, this app helps you manage your financial accounts. However, it also offers personalized advice from financial experts, so you can get a better idea of what your spending habits mean and how to achieve your saving goals.

4. BILLMINDER

If you're responsible for a few bills, then this app is perfect for you! It simplifies the process by keeping your bills in one place, so you know what's due and when.

5. PAYPAL

In today's world, you're likely making more purchases online than in person. Luckily, most online retailers accept PayPal, which can help you make sure that your payments are secure.

6. PRICE PER PINT

So Price Per Pint isn't exactly a finance app, but it'll help you find the cheapest beers near your college. This helps you not only get your money's worth when going out, but also save some serious cash.

7. MOBILE BANKING APPS

This may seem like a no-brainer, but mobile banking apps have come a long way. Many apps will allow you to keep track of recent purchases, deposit checks, and even transfer funds right from your phone.

FIND YOUR PLACE IN THE COLLEGE JOB SCENE

Many students need to find jobs to support themselves or pay for their studies. If you're thinking about applying for a job, research has shown that you're not alone.

College students make up nearly 10 percent of the overall labor force.

A student working full-time at the federal minimum wage would earn $15,080 annually.

of college students are both full-time students and full-time employees.

of undergraduates work at least thirty hours a week.

of employers say they prefer work experience gained through an internship.

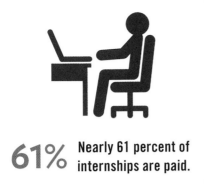

61% Nearly 61 percent of internships are paid.

Unpaid experiences were by far the most common in the social services industry (81.7 percent), followed by education, government, healthcare, and recreation/hospitality (63.9 to 50.4 percent).

14 MILLION
college students work while attending school.

6%

6 percent of college students earn money through work study programs.

61%

61 percent of graduating seniors had an internship or co-op experience.

STUDENT DEBT BY THE NUMBERS

Many people head to college to further their education and to have an opportunity for a better life. While the cost of an education is significant, the majority of students find the value of a college degree to be even more significant. To find out how much it'll cost you, take a look at financial averages across the U.S.

$1,260,000,000,000

IN TOTAL U.S. STUDENT LOAN DEBT.

44.2 MILLION Americans have student loan debt.

The average monthly student loan payment is

$351

The average borrower in 2016 owed

$37,172.

This represents a 6 percent increase from the average debt of 2015 graduates.

68%

of students who graduated in 2015 had student loan debt.

A BREAKDOWN OF THE COST OF COLLEGE

PRIVATE NONPROFIT*

 Tuition and Fees: $33,480

 Books and Supplies: $1,250

 Room and Board: $11,890

 Other Expenses**: $2,720

Total: $49,340

PUBLIC OUT-OF-STATE*

 Tuition and Fees: $24,930

 Books and Supplies: $1,250

 Room and Board: $10,440

 Other Expenses**: $3,270

Total: $39,890

PUBLIC IN-STATE*

 Tuition and Fees: $9,650

 Books and Supplies: $1,250

 Room and Board: $10,440

 Other Expenses**: $3,270

Total: $24,610

*On-campus, four-year
** Transportation, groceries and takeout, entertainment, clothing, and other living expenses

BUDGETING 101

You may not think you need a budget while in school, but it can help you pay your bills and achieve other goals, such as planning an awesome spring break or finally moving off campus. Here's how to create a budget that you'll actually stick to.

1. Establish realistic and measurable financial goals.

Sure, it's great to say that you want to save money, but creating specific goals will help you keep track of your finances better and work toward your desired outcome.

2. Build an emergency fund.

It may seem hard to bank on what-ifs, especially when you don't have a lot of money to begin with, but setting up an emergency fund will come in handy when your car breaks down or you need to pay for extra school supplies.

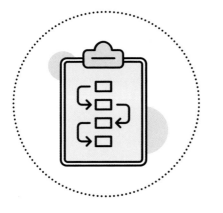

3. Create a monthly spending plan.

Take inventory of all of your monthly spending habits and be sure to factor in your emergency fund. Your plan should include fixed expenses, such as bills and food, as well as wants like eating out and entertainment.

4. Open a savings account.

Again, it may be hard to put money aside for another day, but it's important to start thinking about your future. A savings account will help you work toward bigger financial goals like paying off your loans or buying a new car.

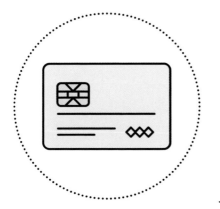

5. Use credit wisely.

If you have a credit card, you'll want to watch your spending and how you pay it off. Good credit can help you later in life when you're looking to buy a home or finance a car.

THE TOP 7 PART-TIME JOBS THAT WILL HELP PAY YOUR BILLS

Chances are good that at some point during your college experience, you'll need a job to help pay for books, meals, or a keg. PayScale recommends the following jobs for college students since they offer part-time hours, don't require a degree, and will help you earn some extra cash. You can also check with the career services department or in the student newspaper for openings in and around your school.

1. RETAIL CASHIER
Median Hourly Salary: $8.97

2. RESTAURANT HOST
Median Hourly Salary: $10.70

3. OFFICE CLERK
Median Hourly Salary: $10.70

4. TUTOR
Median Hourly Salary: $10.70

5. BANK TELLER
Median Hourly Salary: $10.80

6. NANNY
Median Hourly Salary: $12.80

7. DENTAL RECEPTIONIST
Median Hourly Salary: $14.10

THE DOs AND DON'Ts
of Job Hunting

Dedicate every spare moment to your search whether that means writing a cover letter or perusing listings.

Set up an online portfolio that includes your work, resume, and an engaging About Me page.

Network with people at school and in your desired field on LinkedIn.

Be careful about what you post on social media.

Write a customized cover letter, especially for internships or jobs in your field.

If possible, set up interviews when you are at your best, whether that's the morning or afternoon.

Dress professionally for interviews, even if it's for a position at your local coffee shop.

Send a thank-you note after the interview.

Whether you're searching for a part-time job to pay your bills or to gain real-life experience, there are a few things you should know before starting a job hunt. By taking these dos and don'ts into consideration, you can set yourself up for success and show the hiring manager why you're the best person to fill the role.

DON'Ts

Dwell on rejections. They're still opportunities to network and practice interviewing.

Forget to use privacy settings on social media platforms like Facebook and Instagram.

Wear your interview outfit to class or your part-time job. Instead, change into your outfit after your shift or class.

Lose focus on school or your current obligations while searching.

Post your resume on job boards if you're nervous about what your current employer may think.

Allow prospective employers to contact your current job if they don't know you're looking.

Talk negatively about previous employers.

Get discouraged, especially when looking for internships.

BRING YOUR COLLEGE EXPERIENCE FULL CIRCLE WITH AN INTERNSHIP

ON CAMPUS

Approach a professor in your ideal field and ask for her assistance in helping you find an appropriate internship or at least a connection who can.

CONNECT WITH YOUR PROFESSORS

Most career centers offer career counselors as well as a book of the most popular internships for students at that school.

USE YOUR CAREER CENTER AS A RESOURCE

Alumni offices will sometimes help set up internships for undergraduates where they get to work in their desired field and be mentored by an alumnus.

CHECK OUT THE ALUMNI OFFICE

While you'll learn different things throughout the next four years, you should also be thinking about how to gain real-life experience in your desired field. After all, you went to college in order to launch your career, right? Here's how to find the best internship opportunity for you, and bring your education full circle.

OFF CAMPUS

SCOPE OUT LOCAL COMPANIES

If there are companies in your area that sound interesting, take a look at their careers page to see if they're looking for interns.

BUILD A LINKEDIN PROFILE

Create a profile on LinkedIn that highlights your skills and any experience you may have had relating to your desired field. Be sure to network with people you've worked for, and use the platform to search for internships.

RESEARCH PROFESSIONAL ORGANIZATIONS

Some professional organizations will sponsor internships for college students. Visit the website of the association that pertains to your area of study to apply for open positions.

HOW TO RECOVER FROM A SPENDING BINGE

There will likely come a time when you spend a little more than you wanted to. Whether it's because of spring break, splurging on a new outfit, or not factoring in some materials you needed for class, an unexpected spending spree can feel like a huge setback. Luckily, there's still hope for getting your finances back on track.

ASSESS THE DAMAGE.

No one likes seeing how much he or she owes or spent, but it's an important step since it'll give you a better idea of how to move on from the spree.

CREATE A PLAN FOR RECOUPING THE MONEY.

Whether it means strictly sticking to your budget this month and saving any "play" money or using part of your savings to pay off your credit card, you need to build a realistic financial plan that works for your lifestyle.

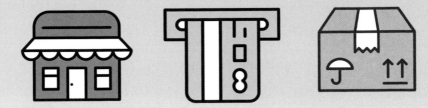

START BOOSTING YOUR INCOME.

Find easy ways to make extra money and start paying off your credit card or replenishing your bank account. You can pick up more shifts at work, sell items online, or offer your services as a freelancer.

CUT BACK ON DAILY SPENDING.

A quick way to get back on track is to cut back on your spending—if only for a few weeks or months. Look for cheaper (or free!) alternatives to your daily routines, such as grabbing coffee instead of a latte, or hosting a night in with friends instead of hitting up the local bar.

DOWNLOAD A BUDGETING APP TO HELP YOU STAY ON TRACK.

If spending sprees are common for you, you may want to download an app to keep track of your habits. Budgeting apps can also help you set up and stick to your financial goals.

Is Grad School for *YOU*?

6 Questions to Ask Yourself Before Making the Decision

While many students jump right into grad school after graduating with a bachelor's degree, getting an advanced degree isn't for everyone. So how do you know if you should start thinking about grad school? These six questions will help you decide if it's the right step for you.

1. *Why do you want to go to grad school?*

Take a look at why you want to go to grad school. Is it because you feel like you chose the wrong major, or do you just dislike the people at your internship? Grad school should be an opportunity to expand your education and get you closer to your desired path.

2. What are your goals?

Continuing your education is a big investment, so you should think about what you want to achieve while in grad school. Are you looking to learn more about a subject you're interested in, or is this education necessary for your dream job?

3. What's the current job market like?

While you may be interested in pursuing a specific career, there may not always be a market for it. Before signing up for grad school, be sure to research your desired field and talk to people in it to really understand where you'd fit in and if the career is actually a viable option.

4. Do your goals outweigh the cost of grad school?

Again, take a look at your goals for grad school and compare it to the cost of getting your master's degree. In some cases, it may be more advantageous to gain real-life experience in your desired field than to continue your education.

5. Can your current finances handle grad school?

Of course, it's important to take a look at your finances before taking on more debt. You'll likely be on your own at this point, so you'll need to pay rent and utilities in addition to any student loans you still have from college.

6. Does your schedule allow for the time commitment?

While there may never be a great time to start grad school, some times are better than others. Be sure that you're ready to commit to another few years of studying, homework, presentations, and tests before applying to grad school.

INDEX

Academic advisor, 45–46
Academic groups, 82–83
Academic pressures, 26–27
Academic success, 43–69
Academic support, 80
Alcohol, drinking, 21, 86–91
Alumni networks, 80, 94, 114
Anxieties, relieving, 25–27
Apartment hunting, 40–41
Art clubs, 82, 85
Attendance policies, 50

Bicycles on campus, 33
Bills, paying, 108–11
Books/supplies, 107
Buddy system, 20–21
Budget, 98–99, 103, 108–9, 116–17
Budget apps, 103, 117

Campus emergency systems, 21
Campus involvement, 72–73,
    82–89
Campus life, 13–41
Campus security, 20–21. See also
    Safety tips
Career centers, 45, 114
Career counselors, 114
Career goals, 44–45, 115, 118–19

Cars on campus, 33
Class participation, 50, 62–63
Class schedules, 46–47
Classes, choosing, 46–47
Classes, missing, 51
Cleaning tips, 30–31
Clothing, packing, 15
Clothing, washing, 22–23
Clubs, 82–83, 85
Cold remedies, 34–35
College costs, 107
College degrees, 37, 74, 110, 118–19
College expenses, 107–9
College graduation, 37, 74, 118
College interviews, 94–95, 97
College jobs, 39, 104–5, 110–13,
    117–19. See also Internships
College policies, 50, 74
College room/board, 107
College scholarships, 94, 96
College shuttles, 33
College tuition, 107
Community service, 78–80, 85
Conflicts, resolving, 17, 76–77
Course catalog, 46
Courses, choosing, 46–47
Credit cards, 100–101, 109, 116–17
Credit rating, 101, 109
Credit report, 101
Cultural events, 39, 82–83, 85, 99

Dating tips, 84–85
De-stressing tips, 25–27
Debt, 106–7, 119
Decorating ideas, 18–19
Degrees, 37, 74, 110, 118–19
Distractions, limiting, 50
Drinking games, 86–87, 89
Drinking responsibly, 21, 90–91

Emergency fund, 108–9
Emergency systems, 21
Entertainment, 32–33, 39, 72–73,
    82–89, 99
Entrance interviews, 94–95, 97
Essays, writing, 58, 94–95. *See also*
    Writing tips
Exam week timeline, 68–69
Exams, acing, 58–59, 68–69
Exams, practicing, 53
Exams, studying, 52
Exercise tips, 24, 26–27
Expenses, 107–9. *See also* Budget

Facebook, 113
Festivals, 82–83
Finance apps, 102–3, 117
Financial aid, 37, 94–97
Financial goals, 108–9, 116–17,
    119
Financial tips, 93–119
Fitness apps, 24
Fitness tips, 24–27, 34–35
Fraternities, 80–81
Freelance services, 117
"Freshman 15," 24–25
Full-time jobs, 104–5. *See also* Jobs

Goals, career, 44–45, 115, 118–19
Goals, financial, 108–9, 116–17, 119
Grad school, 118–19
Grades, improving, 64–65
Graduation, 37, 74, 118
Grants, 94–96
Greek membership, 80–81
Grocery shopping, 33, 98–99

Hazing, 81
Health apps, 24, 27
Healthy snacks, 25, 27
Healthy tips, 24–27, 34–35

Illnesses, 34–35
Improving grades, 64–65
In-state college tuition, 107
Instagram, 113
Internships, 37, 80, 104–5, 112–15,
    118
Interviews, college, 94–95, 97
Interviews, jobs, 112–13
Involvement, 72–73, 82–89

Job hunting tips, 112–13
Job interviews, 112–13
Job market, 119
Job salaries, 104, 110–11
Jobs, 39, 104–5, 110–13, 117–19.
    See also Internships

Laundry tips, 22–23
Lease agreements, 41
Lectures, 50–53

LinkedIn, 112, 115
Living expenses, 107–9. *See also* Budget
Loan applications, 96–97
Loans, 94–97, 106–7

Major, declaring, 44–45
Meals, 24–25, 27
Meditation, 25, 27
Meeting people, 72–73, 89
Minimum wage, 104
Minor, declaring, 44
Money-management apps, 102–3, 117
Money-management tips, 93–119
Money-saving tips, 98–99, 108–9. *See also* Budget
Multiple-choice questions, 59
Music clubs, 82

Networking, 80, 94, 112–15
New friends, 38, 72–73, 89
Nonprofit college tuition, 107
Note-taking tips, 50–53
Nutritional tips, 24–25, 27

Off-campus lifestyles, 40–41
Out-of-state college tuition, 107

Packing tips, 14–15
Papers, writing, 54–55, 58, 66–67. *See also* Writing tips
Part-time jobs, 39, 104–5, 110–13, 117. *See also* Jobs

Parties, attending, 86–87, 89–91
Parties, hosting, 88–89
PayScale, 110
Perkins Loans, 97
Plagiarism, 55
Presentation tips, 60–61
Private college tuition, 107
Professional image, 112
Professional networks, 80, 94, 112–15
Professional organizations, 39, 79, 115
Professional relationships, 62–63
Professors, 50–53, 60–67, 114
Public college tuition, 107
Public transportation, 21, 32–33

Reading skills, enhancing, 48–49
Relationship, with dates, 84–85
Relationship, with new friends, 38, 72–73, 89
Relationship, with professors, 62–63
Relationship, with RA, 17, 74–76
Relationship, with roommate, 16–17, 76–77
Relaxation tips, 25–27
Research papers, writing, 66–67. *See also* Writing tips
Resident Assistant (RA), 17, 74–76
Rideshare services, 32
Room/board, 107
Room cleaning tips, 30–31
Room decorating ideas, 18–19
Room safety tips, 20–21
Roommate conflicts, 17, 76–77
Roommate tips, 16–19, 76–77

Safety tips, 20–21, 81, 90–91
Salaries, 104, 110–11
Savings account, 109
Scholarships, 94, 96
Security system, 20–21
Shopping tips, 33, 98–99, 101
Shuttles, 33
Sleep requirements, 25, 60, 69
Snacks, 25, 27
Social events, 72–73, 80–81, 84–85
Social media, 20–21, 73, 112–13, 115
Social pressures, 26–27
Social skills, 16–17, 71–91
Sororities, 80–81
Spending binge, 116–17
Spending plan, 98–99, 103, 108–9,
    116–17
Sports, 83, 85, 99
Spring break alternatives, 38–39
Spring break, planning, 28–29
Stafford Loans, 97
State college tuition, 107
Stress, reducing, 25–27
Student debt, 106–7, 119
Student government, 83
Student loans, 94–97, 106–7
Study abroad, 36–37
Study groups, 52, 56–57, 65, 68, 80
Study notes, 50–52
Study tools, 52–53
Subsidized loans, 95, 97. *See also*
    Loans
Supplies, choosing, 52–53

Supplies, costs, 107
Supplies, packing, 14–15

Tests, acing, 58–59, 68–69
Tests, practicing, 53
Tests, studying, 52
Thesis, 55, 58, 66. *See also* Writing
    tips
Toiletries, packing, 14
Transportation, 21, 32–33
Transportation apps, 32
Tuition, 107
Tutors, 46, 53, 65, 80, 111

Unsubsidized loans, 95, 97. *See also*
    Loans

Volunteerism, 78–80, 85

Wages, 104, 110–11
Weight gain, 24–27, 34–35
Winter break, 38–39
Work experience, 104–5, 112–15. *See
    also* Internships
Work study programs, 105
Workout tips, 24, 26–27
Writing tips, 54–55, 58, 66–67, 94–95

ABOUT THE AUTHOR

Diane Garcia is a freelance writer and editor with several years of experience working on both digital and print publications. She studied writing and film at Framingham State University. When Diane isn't working, you can find her practicing yoga, hiking, or hanging out with friends. She currently lives in Massachusetts with her partner and her feisty cat, Isaac.

ABOUT THE DESIGNER

Elisabeth Lariviere is an artist and designer who grew up in New England. She studied art and graphic design at the University of Massachusetts Dartmouth, where she discovered her love for printmaking and creating handmade books. When Elisabeth is not designing or creating, she likes to kayak, hike, and camp around the Pacific Northwest; soak in Oregon's amazing hot springs; cook vegan meals for her friends; and fix and ride vintage mopeds. She currently lives in Portland, Oregon, with her adorable dog, Sid.

All other images by Elisabeth Lariviere.